Long Weekend Guide

No business listed in this guide has provided *anything* free to the author.

Andrew Delaplaine

GET 3 FREE NOVELS
Like political thrillers?
See next page to download 3 FREE page-turning
novels—no strings attached.

Senior Editors - ***Renee & Sophie Delaplaine***
Senior Writer - **James Cubby**

Gramercy Park Press
New York London Paris

Copyright © by Gramercy Park Press - All rights reserved.

WANT 3 FREE THRILLERS?
Why, of course you do!
If you like these writers--
Vince Flynn, Brad Thor, Tom Clancy, James Patterson, David Baldacci, John Grisham, Brad Meltzer, Daniel Silva, Don DeLillo
If you like these TV series –
House of Cards, Scandal, West Wing, The Good Wife, Madam Secretary, Designated Survivor

---

You'll love the **unputdownable** series about Jack Houston St. Clair, with political intrigue, romance, and loads of action and suspense.

Besides writing travel books, I've written political thrillers for many years that have delighted hundreds of thousands of readers. I want to introduce you to my work!
Send me an email and I'll send you a link where you can download the first 3 books in my bestselling series, absolutely FREE.
Mention **this book** when you email me.
andrewdelaplaine@mac.com

SAVANNAH
The Delaplaine Long Weekend Guide

TABLE OF CONTENTS

Chapter 1 – WHY SAVANNAH? – 4

Chapter 2 – GETTING ABOUT – 8

Chapter 3 – WHERE TO STAY – 11

Chapter 4 – WHERE TO EAT – 24

Chapter 5 – NIGHTLIFE – 54

Chapter 6 – WHAT TO SEE & DO – 58

Chapter 7 – SHOPPING & SERVICES – 71

INDEX – 91

Other Book by the Author – 95

Chapter 1
WHY SAVANNAH?

Every time I visit Savannah, I ask myself the same question: what is it about this fair city that I like so much?

An impossible question (for me) to answer. The culture? The food (Ah, yes, the food!)? The people? The charming layout of the city?

It's all of those things, of course. Savannah is a much more interesting city than Charleston because you can basically see what there is to see in Charleston in a day. A Long Weekend is more than ample time to savor the riches of Charleston (excluding its numerous fine restaurants) unless you venture to some of the plantations outside town.

Not so Savannah. You'll need a lot more than a Long Weekend to take in everything Savannah has to offer, trust me.

Of all historic figures, Civil War General William Sherman is largely responsible for preserving the city by the simple act of *not* burning it down when he made his famous March to the Sea, destroying everything in his Army's path—except Savannah.

My first experience here was as an undergrad when I came to meet the parents of my college girlfriend. Theirs was one of the older families in Savannah, and their name even graces one of its most famous squares.

Speaking of those famous squares, the layout of Savannah makes it very interesting. There are 21 squares that give this city a strong human scale other U.S. cities will never have. Savannah feels more like London than any other American city to my mind (except of course for the weather). These squares, sometimes frustrating for motorists who have to navigate around them, make cycling around Savannah a pleasure.

There used to be 24 squares in the original plan of the city, but 3 of these were sacrificed to developers who demolished them before the people came to their senses and stopped the wanton destruction of Savannah's valuable heritage. Another square, Ellis, once no more than a parking lot, is now looking more like it did in the old days.

A little side note: famed lyricist Johnny Mercer, who wrote some 1,600 songs and took home 4 Oscars for Best Song, was from here. He was one of the great contributors to the Great American Songbook. (He wrote "Moon River," for example, which Audrey Hepburn sang not so well in "Breakfast at Tiffany's.")

Be certain to visit the **River Street Pedestrian District**. Here you'll see water taxis, riverboats, and numerous private craft plying the river. The waterfront is lined with shops, restaurants and quite a few tourist traps. Still, it's great to see it.

Chapter 2
GETTING ABOUT

CAR
Unless you're going to be staying downtown in the Historic District, you will need a car.

PUBLIC TRANSIT
CAT
Chatham Area Transit
www.catchacat.org
Bus service throughout Savannah. There's a free **CAT Shuttle** (Route #1) that serves the Historic District.

STREETCAR CONNECTONTHEDOT
www.connectonthedot.com
The River Street Streetcar runs 1 mile along an old streetcar line in the Downtown Historic District. It has 12 stops on its route.

FERRY
There's a free **Savannah Belles Ferry** that runs across the Savannah River, linking the Historic District and Convention Center on Hutchinson Island.

WALKING
In the Historic District, you can do a lot of walking. Park your car and go out on foot.

Information:
www.savannahvisit.com

MLK Visitor Information Center
301 Martin Luther King, Jr. Blvd., Savannah, 912-944-0455
www.visit-historic-savannah.com/savannah-visitor-center.html

Tybee Island Visitor Information Center
1st St, Tybee Island, 877-344-3361
www.visittybee.com/travel-aid/tybee-visitor-center

Visitor Center at Ellis Square
26 Barnard St, Savannah, 912-525-3100 x 1343

Savannah/ Hilton Head International Airport Visitor Center
400 Airways Ave, Savannah, 912-966-3743
www.savannahairport.com/at-the-airport/visitor-information-center

Visit Savannah Visitor Information Center
101 E Bay St, Savannah, 912-644-6400
www.visitsavannah.com

The River Street Visitor Information Center
1 W River St, Savannah, 912-651-6662
www.visit-historic-savannah.com/savannah-visitor-center.html

Chapter 3
WHERE TO STAY

DID YOU FIND AN INTERESTING PLACE?
If you discover a place you think I should check out on my next visit, drop me a line, will you? I'll mention your name if I end up listing it.
andrewdelaplaine@mac.com

Savannah has an endless selection of bed-and-breakfasts, including several that are said to be haunted, that range between $200 and $300 a night. The **Association of Historic Inns of Savannah** has listings at www.historicinnsofsavannah.com

THE 17HUNDRED90 INN
307 E President St, Savannah, 912-236-7122
www.17hundred90.com
This historic inn has 14 comfortable rooms, each with king or queen sized bed, private bath, a growing collection of antiques. A stop on most of Savannah's ghost tours and it's said there are ghosts still wandering the rooms.

BALLASTONE
14 E Oglethorpe Ave, Savannah, 912-236-1484
www.ballastone.com

Listed on the National Register of Historic Places, guests feel like they're stepping back to the Victorian era once they enter this beautiful inn that has been elegantly furnished with antiques and fine reproductions. The inn offers 13 guestrooms and 3 suites, all uniquely decorated, some with canopied beds and beamed ceilings. Many rooms have working gas fireplaces and three have whirlpool tubs. Amenities include: Free Wi-Fi, TVs, daily newspapers, morning breakfast, afternoon tea served on fine china, and an evening social hour with hors d'oeuvres. The inn has its own private Victorian bar fully stocked with boutique wines.

BOHEMIAN HOTEL
102 W Bay St, Savannah, 912-721-3800
www.bohemianhotelsavannah.com
Here the old meets the new as design elements celebrate the 18th century era but with modern luxuries. Amenities include: concierge services, fitness center, 37-inch LCD TVs, and complimentary wireless Internet access. Rooms feature Historic District or Riverfront views. This is a pet-friendly and smoke-free hotel. On-site restaurant and lounge featuring live music.

THE BRICE
601 E Bay St, Savannah, 912-238-1200
www.bricehotel.com
The elegant Brice Hotel, shiny as a new penny, features 145 guestrooms including 26 suites. Big floor-to-ceiling windows look out over Washington Square. The 1860s building has almost as storied a

history as Savannah itself. It's been a cotton warehouse, Coca-Cola bottling plant, a stable, among other things. It's a Kimpton property, so you can be sure it's a fun and lively place to stay, with a whimsical ambience and playful designs. Here you'll be welcomed with Southern hospitality and enjoy the lavish extras one would expect from a grand old Savannah hotel. Amenities include: outdoor pool fringed with palm trees, free bikes, free coffee and tea in the lobby every morning (and free wine daily at the cocktail hour), in-room spa services available, free Wi-Fi, flat-screen TVs with cable channels, and iPod docks. Smoke-free hotel. On-site bar/lounge, the **Pacci Italian Kitchen & Bar**, is a large open space, serving items like Cola glazed short ribs with mushroom risotto. Pet friendly hotel.

EAST BAY INN
225 E. Bay St., 800-500-1225
www.eastbayinn.com

The rooms here at this B&B tend to be a little larger than you see elsewhere. Some rooms have 4-posters, others have two large queen size beds, some are pet-friendly. Lots of great moldings and dark woods that really give you the feel you're in an old Victorian mansion. (The creaky floors do, too!) Free newspapers in the morning, bellman service, breakfast in the morning—they offer a lot of extras touches you'll appreciate.

FOLEY HOUSE INN
14 Hull St, Savannah, 800 647 3708
www.foleyinn.com
This authentic bed and breakfast inn offers a variety of room options; all 19-guest rooms are uniquely decorated to complement the time and historical heritage. Amenities include: complimentary breakfast, afternoon sweets and tea, evening wine and hors d'oeuvres, complimentary morning paper and comfy cotton bathrobes. This is a perfect setting for a romantic getaway. Conveniently located near the Historic District, shopping, and other local attractions. All rooms are non-smoking.

THE GALLOWAY HOUSE B&B
107 E. 35th St, Savannah, 912-658-4419
www.thegallowayhouse.com
Located in the heart of the Historical District, this charming three-level Bed & Breakfast offers private 1 or 2 bedroom apartments. Amenities include: unlimited breakfast in your apartment whenever you choose, complimentary secure Wi-Fi, and HDTV with DIRECTV. Pet friendly.

HOTEL TYBEE
1401 Strand Ave, Tybee Island, 912-786-7777
www.hoteltybee.com
If you'd rather be near the expansive beaches on Tybee Island than in the middle of the Historic District, this resort features 208 rooms and suites on the beach near Tybee Pier. Rooms are spacious and many have private balconies. Dine on-site at A-J's Beachside Restaurant and Bar specializing in fresh seafood with a Southern twist.

KEHOE HOUSE
123 Habersham St., 912-232-1020
www.kehoehouse.com
Built in 1893 for William Kehoe of Kehoe Ironworks. What looks like white wooden trim is actually iron. Located in the Historic District, this exquisitely restored 1892 mansion offers 13 guestrooms all decorated with elegant furnishings and antiques. Amenities include: Cooked-to-order breakfast, wine and hors d'oeuvres reception, homemade desserts & coffee service, 24-hour concierge, CD & DVD players, wireless internet, and turndown service. An Adults-Only B&B.

MANSION ON FORSYTH PARK
700 Drayton St., Savannah: 912-238-5158
www.mansiononforsythpark.com
This Victorian mansion dating back to 1888 is located in the heart of Savannah's Historic District has over 100 rooms, and they've crammed all the amenities of

a full-scale resort into them. You've got a fabulous spa, a cooing school, an art gallery boasting over 400 pieces by today's artists. And let's not overlook its fine restaurant, **700 Drayton**. Even if you're not staying here, it's a good idea to go to the rooftop **Casimir's Lounge** for a drink on the terrace overlooking the Historic District. (Live jazz and blues Fri & Sat nights.)

THE MARSHALL HOUSE
123 E Broughton St, Savannah, 912-644-7896
www.marshallhouse.com
Savannah's oldest hotel, built in 1851 and restored in 1999. The hotel has 68 rooms, some with antique clawfoot tubs and access to a wrought-iron balcony.

MONTAGE AT PALMETTO BLUFF
477 Mount Pelia Rd, Bluffton, 843-706-6500
www.montagehotels.com/palmettobluff/

This inn (a bit out of town from Savannah) offers charming cottages and village homes surrounding the Inn on 20,000 acres of property overlooking the May River. You stsy in one of the cottages but the focal point is the Inn itself where you can enjoy shrimp and grits for breakfast. You zip around in golf carts. Amenities offered include: outdoor pool, lap pool, and spa facility. Variety of outdoor activities available for guests. On-site fine dining.

PLANTERS INN
29 Abercorn St, Savannah, 912-232-5678 or 800-554-1187
www.plantersinnsavannah.com
Located in downtown Savannah, this elegant hotel offers extravagant amenities and beautifully appointed rooms. Amenities include: free wine & cheese social, nightly turndown service, expanded continental breakfast delivered to your room, free USA Today newspapers, digital cable/satellite TV, free wireless internet access, and free bottled water. Conveniently located near the Historic District and attractions like the Telfair Museum of the Arts, Gordon Low House, River Street and City Market. Guests enjoy dining at The Olde Pink House, one of Savannah's most popular restaurants, located next door to the Planters Inn.

PRESIDENTS' QUARTERS INN
225 E President St, Savannah, 912-233-1600
www.presidentsquarters.com
This historic boutique hotel offers 16 richly appointed suites – some featuring balconies overlooking the

courtyard, decorated in antique and period reproduction furniture. Amenities include: Free gourmet breakfast, afternoon hors d'oeuvres, cable TV, free Wi-Fi, and free on-site parking.

RIVER STREET INN
124 E. Bay St., Savannah, 912-234-6400
www.riverstreetinn.com
The River Street Inn, located at the beginning of Savannah's Landmark district, is an intimate 86-room guest hotel that overlooks the Savannah River. Guests are treated to the charm of the past mixed with modern conveniences and personal amenities. Guest rooms feature private baths with brass bath fixtures, exquisite furnishings and hardwood floors. Amenities

include: free morning newspaper, afternoon wine & hors d'oeuvres reception, homemade chocolates as you retire for the evening, free coffee, in-room movies, data port & Wi-Fi. Conveniently located near Savannah's Historic District, local attractions, museums, antique shops, shopping, and restaurants. 100% non-smoking hotel. Four on-site restaurants, and variety of on-site shopping.

SAVANNAH BED AND BREAKFAST INN
121 W Gordon St, Savannah, 912-238-0518
www.savannahbnb.com
This historic inn is within walking distance to all attractions. The Inn features 15 air-conditioned guestrooms and three cottages.

THE THUNDERBIRD INN
611 W Oglethorpe Ave, Savannah, 912-232-2661
www.thethunderbirdinn.com
A no-frills motel recently refurbished. Conveniently located near attractions like the Telfair Museum of Art, Thunderbird offers 42 air-condition guestrooms. Amenities include: free wireless Internet access, TVs with premium cable channels, free breakfast, and tour/ticket assistance. This is a smoke-free property. Southern hospitality perks include Moon Pies on guests' pillows and Krispy Kreme donuts delivered hot at dawn.

THE WESTIN SAVANNAH HARBOR GOLF RESORT & SPA
1 Resort Drive, Savannah, 912-201-2000
www.westinsavannah.com

This resort and spa is a mixture of modern luxury and Southern charm. Located directly across the river from the heart of the Historic District. To get over, they have a free 2-minute ferry ride that takes you to River Street. The great advantage of staying here, of course, is that you're close to the Historic District, but you have all the modern amenities you won't find in your typical B&B. They have an 18-hole PGA golf course, the **Heavenly Spa** and there's also a beautiful pool and beach club. There's a pool bar and grill, a lounge, and the **Aqua Star** features award-winning seafood cuisine from Chef Roger Michel.

Chapter 4
WHERE TO EAT

DID YOU FIND AN INTERESTING PLACE?
If you discover a place you think I should check out on my next visit, drop me a line, will you? I'll mention your name if I end up listing it.
andrewdelaplaine@mac.com

45 BISTRO
123 E Broughton St, Savannah, 912-234-3111
www.45bistro.com
CUISINE: American
DRINKS: Full Bar
SERVING: Dinner
PRICE RANGE: $$$
Located adjacent to the historic Marshall House, here you'll enjoy some of Savannah's finest dining. Chef Ryan Behneman prepares dishes like lasagna of jumbo sea scallops, wilted spinach, mascarpone cheese and a tomato ragu and filet of salmon gratinéed with sautéed hearts of palm and artichokes.

700 DRAYTON
Mansion on Forsyth Park
700 Drayton St., Savannah: 912-721-5002
www.mansiononforsythpark.com
The she-crab bisque here has lumps of crab meat and they aren't shy with the sherry. While they have a fine selection of steaks here, I'd focus on the Southern specialties: crispy chicken livers, pan-fried crab cakes, shrimp fritters, things of this sort, because they do such a good job.

A-J's DOCKSIDE RESTAURANT
1315 Chatham Ave, Tybee Island, 912-786-9533
www.ajsdocksidetybee.com
CUISINE: Seafood
DRINKS: Full Bar
SERVING: Dinner
PRICE RANGE: $$
Tucked into a quiet waterfront corner on the island's south side. Here you'll find some of the best seafood on the island. Try favorites like the shrimp and grits or artichoke dip appetizers, or a bowl of crab stew or scored flounder. Arrive early for dinner.

ATLANTIC
102 E Victory Dr., Savannah, 912-417-8887
www.atlanticsavannah.com
CUISINE: American (New)
DRINKS: Full Bar
SERVING: Dinner; Closed Sundays
PRICE RANGE: $$
Located in what used to be a gas station dating back to the 1930s, this is a popular eatery that offers a menu of New American fare in a bright and airy room with massive amounts of light streaming through the high windows. There's a patio out front and another in the back. Or you can eat at the bar. There are several large plates suitable for sharing. Favorites: Pork Belly with a rich flavorful succotash; Beet (not Beef) carpaccio; and Grilled Cheese with a small cup of Curry tomato soup served in a Campbell soup can. (I know, it's gimmicky, but it's good!) Impressive wine selection. Reservations recommended.

BACK IN THE DAY BAKERY
2403 Bull St, Savannah, 912-495-9292
www.backinthedaybakery.com
An old-fashioned bakery that's a favorite among locals, tourists and foodies. Not just a bakery but also a café with a delicious menu of sandwiches, like the Madras curry chicken on ciabatta. Here you'll find Savannah's best desserts, artisan breads, award winning cupcakes along with great coffee and espresso. Free Wifi.

BOAR'S HEAD GRILL & TAVERN
1 N Lincoln St, Savannah, 912-651-9660
www.boarsheadgrillandtavern.com
CUISINE: American
DRINKS: Full Bar
SERVING: Lunch & Dinner

PRICE RANGE: $$
Located in the historic section of Savannah, Chef Philip Branan prepares a delicious selection of steaks, chops and seafood.

CLARY'S CAFÉ
404 Abercorn St, Savannah, 912-233-0402
www.claryscafe.com
Steeped in local history, Clary's, in business since 1903, serves breakfast all day including omelets, grits, steaming biscuits and plain, pecan strawberry and blueberry malted waffles. The restaurant is covered with knickknacks, paintings, family pictures and memorabilia.

DECK BEACH BAR AND KITCHEN
404 Butler Ave., Tybee Island, 912-328-5397
www.thedecktybee.com
CUISINE: American (New)/Seafood
DRINKS: Full Bar
SERVING: Lunch & Dinner; Closed Mon – Wed.
PRICE RANGE: $$
Less than a half-hour from Savannah, this is the only bar / restaurant on the sand in Tybee with ocean views from every seat. Favorites: Vietnamese style shrimp Po Boy sandwich and Chicken Satay sandwich. The seafood platter here is big enough to satisfy 2 or even 3. It's tempura cod made with a beer-batter, grilled shrimp, fried calamari, snow crab legs, ahi tuna poke (they say it's ahi tuna, but probably not), corn on the cob, vinegar fries, sweet

potato fries and a good portion of island-style cole slaw. (I was with one other person when we ordered it, and we brought home enough to feed another person.) The good thing about this seafood platter is that it's not all fried, like so many others. Vegetarian options. Dining inside or on the deck. Happy hour. The view makes this a great brunch spot. Go for a walk on the beach to work up an appetite. (Note the closed days above.)

ELIZABETH ON 37TH
105 E 37th St, Savannah, 912-236-5547
www.elizabethon37th.net
CUISINE: American
DRINKS: Full Bar
SERVING: Dinner
PRICE RANGE: $$$

Chef Kelly Yambor serves up fresh seafood in an elegant stately mansion dating back to the early 20th Century. Favorites include the shrimp and grits with red-eye gravy, traditionally made from leftover coffee, Bluffton oysters served three ways, including raw with tomato-cilantro; snapper with a chewy crust of shredded potato and asiago cheese; spicy red rice & shrimp; clams with roasted Vidalia onions. They use house grown herbs and edible flowers in their dishes. There's a 7-course tasting menu available that's a good bet. Excellent service from beginning to end.

EMPORIUM KITCHEN AND WINE MARKET
254 E Perry St., Savannah, 912-559-8400
www.emporiumsavannah.com
CUISINE: American (New)

DRINKS: Full Bar
SERVING: Breakfast, Lunch, & Dinner
PRICE RANGE: $$
Popular eatery offering locally sourced, quality menu items, but it's also part market, part coffee shop, a bistro-style feel to it and a take-away option. Favorites: Local Salmon en Papillote; Roasted BBQ oysters; and Rabbit Ragout with House-Made Pappardelle. Bar on first floor and rooftop, ice cream bar and wine area, and games on rooftop.

FLYING MONK NOODLE BAR
5 W Broughton St, Savannah, 912-232-8888
www.flywiththemonk.com
CUISINE: Vietnamese
DRINKS: Beer & Wine Only
SERVING: Lunch & Dinner
PRICE RANGE: $$
This popular eatery offers a menu restaurant featuring pan-Asian noodle dishes. Noodle dishes from a variety of Asian nations are represented including Vietnam, Malaysia, China, Thailand, Korea, and Laos. Menu favorites include: Pho beef and Peking Duck.

FOXY LOXY CAFÉ
1919 Bull St, Savannah, 912-401-0543
www.foxyloxycafe.com
CUISINE: Espresso Bar/Tex-Mex
DRINKS: Beer & Wine
SERVING: Breakfast, Lunch, Desserts
PRICE RANGE: $

A cute little place with a small menu but they serve excellent craft beers and delicious tacos. There's also a nice dessert selection, great coffees and they serve breakfast all day. Live music on Tuesday nights.

GREEN FIRE PIZZA
236 Drayton St., Savannah, 912-298-0880
www.greenfirepizza.com
CUISINE: Neapolitan-style Pizza / Chicken Wings
DRINKS: Beer & Wine Only
SERVING: Lunch & Dinner, Lunch only on Saturdays
PRICE RANGE: $$
Modern pizzeria with creative Italian dishes, but with an emphasis on the pizza coming out of the 800-degree wood burning oven they imported from Italy. Known for their Garlic Knots (I guarantee that your mouth will get that wonderful garlic burn that drives me cray with pleasure). You can "create your own pizza" choosing from a list of over 20 toppings. But

the ones they've already created are pretty damn impressive: like the Giardino (Calabrian chile pesto, broccolini, cherry tomatoes and sausage). Favorites: Arugula salad and the Smokin' Green Fire Pizza. Outdoor seating and bar area.

GREEN TRUCK PUB
2430 Habersham St., 912-234-5885
www.greentruckpub.com
CUISINE: Pubs, Burgers
DRINKS: Beer & Wine
SERVING: Lunch, dinner, Tuesday-Saturday
PRICE RANGE: $$
The crew at the Green Truck Pub, just a parking lot away from the Habersham antiques mall, makes simple food from scratch, sourcing as many of their ingredients as they can locally. They use grass-fed beef from Hunter Cattle in nearly Brooklet, and their pork and free-range chicken are raised in Georgia. They buy their coffee beans from Perc Coffee just a

few blocks away. Produce is selected at the farmer's market at nearby Forsyth Park. Popular menu items include the Rustico burger with goat cheese, balsamic caramelized onions, roasted red peppers and fresh basil that they grow in their backyard garden; the Whole Farm, a bacon-cheddar burger topped with a fried egg; the California BLT has avocado; one of my favorites here is the Grilled Cheese with bacon and tomato. Add the hand-cut fries and you're all set. They have a rotating selection of about 30 craft beers.

THE GREY
109 Martin Luther King Jr Blvd, Savannah, 912-662-5999
www.thegreyrestaurant.com
CUISINE: American (New) / Bistro
DRINKS: Full Bar
SERVING: Lunch & Dinner; closed Mon
PRICE RANGE: $$$
Located in a sleek refurbished 1938 Greyhound bus depot from the Art Deco era, this high-end eatery offers a pleasing menu of Southern fare from Chef Mashama Bailey. The kitchen was installed in what used to be the ticket booth. Fancy décor with steel-blue booths, terrazzo floors. There was a 24-hour diner in the old bus station that has been remodeled into an elegant bar. The chef was born in the Bronx, but has steeped herself in Southern cuisine. Try her spicy BBQ sauce she slathers on her chicken schnitzel sandwich. Nice wine list with a focus on European labels. This is a good place to begin a night on the town.

GRYPHON TEA ROOM
337 Bull St., Savannah, 912-525-5880
www.scadgryphon.com
CUISINE: Tea Room/American fare
DRINKS: No Booze
SERVING: Lunch & Dinner
PRICE RANGE: $
American café known for their sumptuous tea service that's situated on the wonderful Madison Square in the handsome Scottish Rite Masonic Temple that dates back to 1926. Gryphon is part of the Savannah

College of Art & Design. Though they have a great short menu, including delectable sandwiches, the tea is what you'll want to come here for. Impressive selection of teas served with tea sandwiches, scones and Devonshire cream & jam. That said, I might add they have an excellent brunch menu as well, with a full English breakfast which includes a sweet potato hash that's out of this world. Favorites: Asian-marinated salmon and Maple-glazed pork loin. There's outdoor seating on the red-bricked sidewalk.

HUSK
12 W Oglethorpe Ave., Savannah, 912-349-2600
www.husksavannah.com
CUISINE: Southern/Desserts

DRINKS: Full Bar
SERVING: Lunch & Dinner
PRICE RANGE: $$

Set in a landmark mansion, this elegant eatery offers a menu of Southern fare, but with a unique twist shared by its other outposts in Charleston and Nashville (among other cities). They strive to use the "indigenous ingredients" of coastal Georgia. And they do it so well. As a rule, the first meal I eat when I get to Charleston is at Husk. Now the same is true in Savannah. Menu changes daily, depending on what's available that's fresh and in season. Favorites: Hot Fried Chicken with Bradford Collards; Glazed pork ribs with pickled Georgia peaches (those peaches are SO good); and Mark's Tilefish. Order a side of sour dough bread for the table – you won't be disappointed. Upstairs bar. Nice wine selection.

Interior of HUSK – just one of the rooms

THE LADY AND SONS
102 W Congress St, Savannah, 912-233-2600
www.ladyandsons.com
CUISINE: Southern
DRINKS: Full bar
SERVING: Lunch and dinner daily
PRICE RANGE: $$-$$$
This is the place that launched Paula Deen, the place that inspired her first cookbook that led to stardom on the Food Network. Always a busy place. The sons mentioned are Jamie and Bobby. This 3-floor complex serves some 8,000 or 9,000 people a week. Three separate tour groups offer Paula Deen tours that will take visitors to her restaurant and the one she operates with her brother on Tybee Island as well as some other Deen-related stops. The menu is extensive, one of those "something for everything" kind of menus you see at a national chain. And I don't

particularly like the place because you feel like one of the cattle that end up in the burgers when you come here. This is not to say the food is less than good: crab cakes, crab stuffed Portobello, fried green tomatoes, black pepper shrimp, fried okra, crab stew cup. There's even an all you can eat Southern Buffet. I do, however, stop in often to buy things from their store. (People love things I get here as gifts.)

LOCAL 11 TEN FOOD & WINE
1110 Bull St, Savannah, 912-790-9000
www.local11ten.com
CUISINE: New Southern
DRINKS: Full bar (excellent wine list)
SERVING: Dinner nightly from 6
PRICE RANGE: $$
Though the building is in an unassuming structure that used to be a bank a block from Forsyth Park, inside you'll find an elegant room with sky-high ceilings, blond paneled walls. The people here insist on listing the farms where the vegetables came from, the company that delivered fish caught that day, the cheesemonger who produced their cheeses, the guy who cured their bacon, the company that made their grits. Maybe they push this element too hard, but the results speak for themselves. They *care* about their

food. Try the Caesar's salad here: made with local romaine lettuce, pecorino Romano, olives, bacon bits and their own croutons. You've never had a Caesar's salad like this. The charcuterie board features meats they cured themselves and even their own pickles. Main courses might include frog legs from North Carolina or Beaufort County octopus with shaved onion and marinated feta, or, one night I was there, I had the milk-braised lamb's belly. Boy, was it tender. Menu changes frequently. Bright idea: do the chef's tasting menu and enjoy the tour. (Wine list here is very good, by the way, one of the best in town.)

MASADA CAFÉ
2301 W Bay St, Savannah, 912-236-9499
No Website
CUISINE: Southern
DRINKS: No Booze
SERVING: Lunch

PRICE RANGE: $
Located in the United House of Prayer for All People, so you know the food is prepared with love. Here

you'll find no frills Southern cooking and it's all about good home cooked soul food. Order from a simple menu that includes crispy fried chicken, delicious mac 'n cheese, and sweet potatoes served with cinnamon and nutmeg. For the entire experience visit the 11 a.m. Sunday service then stay for lunch.

MRS. WILKES' DINING ROOM
107 W Jones St, Savannah, 912-232-5997
www.mrswilkes.com
CUISINE: Southern / Soul Food
DRINKS: No Booze
SERVING: Lunch – weekdays; closed Sat & Sun
PRICE RANGE: $$
This busy Southern diner offers a family experience as lunch guests dine at communal tables. Tables are

covered with dishes like Fried chicken, sweet potato soufflé, black-eyed peas, okra gumbo, corn muffins and biscuits. Menu changes daily.

OLDE PINK HOUSE
23 Abercorn St, Savannah, 912-232-4286
www.plantersinnsavannah.com/the-olde-pink-house/
CUISINE: Southern
DRINKS: Full Bar
SERVING: Lunch, Dinner
PRICE RANGE: $$$

If you love Southern cooking then you must eat here, as the food is to die for. Menu favorites include: Fried Green Tomatoes and the Shrimp & Grits. The setting is lovely and each part of the house has a historical theme. Save room for dessert and have the Chocolate Mouse Bomb.

PACCI ITALIAN KITCHEN + BAR @ THE BRICE HOTEL
601 E Bay St, Savannah, 912-233-6002
www.paccisavannah.com
CUISINE: Italian
DRINKS: Full Bar
SERVING: Breakfast, Lunch & Dinner
PRICE RANGE: $$
This rustic restaurant/bar offers Chef Roberto Leoci's menu of locally sourced Italian cuisine. Menu favorites include: Prosciutto and Melon and Cubano Italiano – a delicious pasta dish.

RANCHO ALEGRE CUBAN
402 Martin Luther King Jr Blvd, Savannah, 912-292-1656

www.ranchoalegrecuban.com
CUISINE: Cuban/Seafood
DRINKS: Full Bar
SERVING: Lunch & Dinner
PRICE RANGE: $$

No frills but pleasant enough Cuban eatery serving traditional plates of Cuban, Caribbean, Spanish and Latin American fare. (So much for focus.) Favorites: Marinated steak and Paella (if you want Paella put in your order right away as it takes 40 minutes—the Paella here is prepared Valenciana style—quite delicious and bursting with flavors). Creative cocktails. The "Suicide" cocktail is deadly, LOL. Latin Jazz on the weekends. Wines from the Argentine, since Cuba is mostly known for beer, daiquiris, mojitos, 1950s cars with new engines and lots and lots of potholes. Oh, and outdated Communism.

SANDFLY BBQ
8413 Ferguson Ave, Savannah, 912-356-5463

www.sandflybbq.com
CUISINE: Barbeque
DRINKS: Beer & Wine Only
SERVING: Lunch & Dinner; closed Sun
PRICE RANGE: $$
A popular eatery serving Savannah style BBQ. Here you can sample delicious BBQ sandwiches, combination plates and smoked meats – glorious Southern fare. Excellent ribs and baked beans. The menu also includes a variety of specials of Southwestern, Cajun, and Creole cuisine.

SENTIENT BEAN
13 E Park Ave, Savannah, 912-232-4447
www.sentientbean.com
CUISINE: Vegetarian
DRINKS: No Booze
SERVING: Breakfast, Lunch & Dinner (7 a.m. to 10 p.m.)

PRICE RANGE: $
This coffee shop is a treat to visit and the menu if filled with organic, homemade food. This is a vegetarian/vegan's delight serving fresh, local organic foods. Menu consists of salads, tortillas, sandwiches and homemade soups. Breakfast served all day. There's also live music, film, and open mic nights. Check out the website for the rotating schedule.

SIX PENCE PUB
245 Bull St, Savannah, 912-233-3151
www.sixpencepub.com
CUISINE: American Traditional
DRINKS: Full Bar
SERVING: Lunch & Dinner
PRICE RANGE: $$
Those favoring British-style pubs will feel at home here. The pub eats are strictly English fare and the beer selection is quite impressive.

SOHO SOUTH CAFÉ
12 W Liberty St, Savannah, 912-233-1633
www.sohosouthcafe.com
CUISINE: American
DRINKS: Beer & Wine Only
SERVING: Lunch
PRICE RANGE: $$
This funky café, located in a former auto repair garage, is operated by local artists. Menu includes dishes like eggs Savannah, an English muffin topped with a jumbo crab cake, poached egg, asparagus and béarnaise. Their slogan, and it's appropriate, is "Where Food is Art.'"

SUNDAE CAFÉ
304 First St., Tybee Island, 912-786-7694
www.sundaecafe.com
WEBSITE DOWN AT PRESSTIME
CUISINE: Reinvented Southern
DRINKS: Full bar
SERVING: Lunch, Dinner
PRICE RANGE: $$
Fried green tomatoes are in lots of dishes of this family-owned Tybee Island restaurant: you can get them as an appetizer or on top of salad, a BLT or even a burger. Other favorites: seafood cheesecake, shrimp and grits and a variety of other seafood. Paula Deen is said to like the double-cut pork chop. Speaking of Deen, she's added their recipes for Succotash, Apple Chutney and Buttermilk Biscuit Blue Cheese Bread Pudding in her "Cooking with Paula Deen" magazine.

VINNIE VAN GO-GO'S
317 W Bryan St, Savannah, 912-233-6394

www.vinnievangogo.com
CUISINE: Pizza
DRINKS: Beer & Wine Only
SERVING: Lunch & Dinner
PRICE RANGE: $
This popular indoor-outdoor pizza joint offers hearty crust pizza.

WALL'S BARBECUE
515 E York Ln, Savannah, 912-232-9754
No Website
CUISINE: Barbeque, Soul Food
DRINKS: No Booze
SERVING: Lunch & Dinner; has erratic operating hours, but usually open weekends

PRICE RANGE: $
An out-of-the-way eatery is prized by locals. They only have 3 tables or so but the food is just fine. Thick crab cakes, plates of crab, chicken, fish or pork served with sides of rice, coleslaw, collard greens or okra. The deviled crab is good, and the ribs are excellent, too.

WYLD DOCK BAR
2740 Livingston Ave, Savannah, 912-692-1219
http://www.thewylddockbar.com/
CUISINE: Seafood
DRINKS: Full Bar
SERVING: Lunch & Dinner; Closed Mondays
PRICE RANGE: $$
Waterside eatery serving New American fare about 15 or 20 minutes from Savannah where you'll get an expansive view of marshlands. Fresh seafood daily. Menu changes often, usually every month. Try the Fresh catch and Fish tacos served in banana leaves; Quail & Rabbit Sausage; Shrimp roll. Outdoor dining

with waterfront views of the desolate marshlands. Locals' hangout.

ZUNZI'S
108 E York St, Savannah, 912-443-9555
www.zunzis.com
CUISINE: International/Sandwiches
DRINKS: No Booze
SERVING: Lunch
PRICE RANGE: $
Closed Sunday
This café offers a mixture of international cuisine (Swiss, Italian, South African, and Dutch). Menu favorites include: The Godfather (an amazing

sandwich made of smoked sausage, chicken, cheese, lettuce and tomato) and the Portabella Sandwich. Ideal for a casual lunch on a nice day.

Chapter 5
NIGHTLIFE

DID YOU FIND AN INTERESTING PLACE?
If you discover a place you think I should check out on my next visit, drop me a line, will you? I'll mention your name if I end up listing it.
andrewdelaplaine@mac.com

AMERICAN LEGION SAVANNAH POST NO 135
1108 Bull St, Savannah, 912-233-9277
www.alpost135.com

A historic structure that was built in 1913, now houses the town's neighborhood bar. No frills bar with cheap drinks.

**CASIMIR'S LOUNGE
MANSION ON FORSYTH PARK**
700 Drayton St., Savannah: 912-721-5002
www.mansiononforsythpark.com
Try to squeeze in a drink at Casimir's, the rooftop lounge above the Mansion on Forsyth Park where you can look out over the Historic District. (Live jazz and blues Fri & Sat nights.) Always a real treat whenever I visit Savannah.

CLUB ONE
1 Jefferson St, Savannah, 912-232-0200

www.clubone-online.com
The site of The Lady Chablis Show until her passing in September 2016. The club still offers cabaret with a variety of performers. Cash only.

CRYSTAL BEER PARLOR
301 W Jones St, Savannah, 912-349-1000
www.crystalbeerparlor.com
This is Savannah's second oldest restaurant and a favorite gathering spot for locals. Simple menu but everything is fresh and prepared to order. Friendly servers and great selection of beers.

PLANTERS TAVERN
23 Abercorn St, Savannah, 912-232-4286
www.plantersinnsavannah.com
A dimly lit, low-ceilinged bar in the basement of the high-dollar Olde Pink House, a dignified restaurant in a 1771 house. There's dining room upstairs but downstairs is where all the action is. If you get a seat by the fireplace you might want decide to stay all night and enjoy the live music.

Chapter 6
WHAT TO SEE & DO

DID YOU FIND AN INTERESTING PLACE?
If you discover a place you think I should check out on my next visit, drop me a line, will you? I'll mention your name if I end up listing it.
andrewdelaplaine@mac.com

ANDREW LOW HOUSE
329 Abercorn St, Savannah, 912-233-6854
www.andrewlowhouse.com

The Andrew Low House, overlooking Lafayette Square, is an Italianate-style stucco building that gives visitors a little insight into life in Savannah more than 150 years ago. Andrew Low's daughter-in-law, Juliette Gordon Low, founded the Girl Scouts of the USA in the parlor and died in the house in 1927 making the house a popular destination for Girl Scout troops. Visitors can tour the restored house that features 13-foot ceilings, period antiques, crystal chandeliers, Egyptian marble fireplaces and giant mahogany doors.

BATTLEFIELD PARK HERITAGE CENTER
300 Martin Luther King Blvd, Savannah, 912-651-6840
https://www.savannah.com/battlefield-park/
This Park is a memorial to the soldiers who fought and died for freedom. Battlefield Park commemorates the second bloodiest battle of the Revolutionary War on October 9, 1779. The **Roundhouse Railroad Museum** (now called the Georgia State Railroad Museum) is also located here with one of the nation's best surviving examples of pre-Civil War railroad structures.

BLUE ORB TOURS
22 W Bryan St, Savannah, 912-665-4258
www.blueorbtours.com
Founded in 2010, this tour is a great way to see haunted Savannah. They offer four different tours: Grave Tales Ghost Tour, Beyond Good and Evil Tour, Adults Only Dead of Night Ghost Tour and

Ghost City Haunted Pub Crawl. Tours are fun and more entertaining than scary but the guides are great storytellers. Times and rates vary depending on the tour.

BULL RIVER MARINA
8005 E US Hwy 80, Savannah, 912-897-7300
www.bullrivermarina.com

This small marina offers boat charters, fishing, rafting, and kayaking. Just a simple old building with old boats and cool guys running the place. Rent a boat (with a captain) and go out to view the sunset.

FLANNERY O'CONNOR'S CHILDHOOD HOME
207 East Charlton St, Savannah, 912-233-6014
www.flanneryoconnorhome.org
This museum is housed in the former childhood home of acclaimed novelist and short story writer Flannery O'Conner. This house is restored to the Depression-era and guided tours of the home are available. Guests can view rare books in the Bruckeimer Library. The gift shop offers unique books and gifts. Free events are offered during the year including the Sunday lecture series. Open Fri through Wednesday. Closed Thursdays. Nominal admission fee.

FORSYTH PARK
Drayton Street, Savannah, 912-651-6610,
www.savannah.com/parks-savannah
Forsyth Park is a beautiful 30-acre city park located in Savannah's Historic District. Filled with magnificent oak and magnolia trees, the park features include walking paths, a café, a huge 19th-century fountain of trumpeting mermen and spouting swans, a Confederate Memorial Statue, two well-equipped playgrounds, and vast lawns often used for soccer and Frisbee. The park is also the site of free concerts.

FORT PULASKI NATIONAL MONUMENT
US Hwy 80 E, Savannah, 912-786-5787
www.nps.gov/fopu/index.htm

Fort Pulaski, located between Savannah and Tybee Island, is an enormous Civil War-era fort that once guarded Savannah. The Fort, a fine example of historic military architecture, acts as a large-scale outdoor exhibit featuring demilune, drawbridges, ditches, and dikes. An inside exhibit shows the history of Fort Pulaski. Visitors can participate in a variety of outdoor activities including hiking, biking, fishing, and bird watching.

GEORGIA STATE RAILROAD MUSEUM
655 Louisville Rd, Savannah, 912-651-6823
www.chsgeorgia.org/GSRM
A National Historic Landmark, the Roundhouse Railroad Museum is the oldest and largest existing nineteenth-century operations complex in the U.S. On display are passenger cars, steam and diesel locomotives, steam-powered machinery, model

railroads, and a 126-foot brick smokestack. Thirteen of the original structures remain.

HEARSE TOURS
412 E Duffy St, Savannah, 912-695-1578
www.hearseghosttours.com
There's no better way to experience a Ghost Tour than riding in a hearse. An open-top hearse can pick you up at your hotel for this special Hearse Ghost Tour. On this tour you'll see some of Savannah's beautiful mansions and drive through the Historic District. You'll also hear about some of Savannah's most notorious murders, suicides, and deathbed tales. Ghost tours are very popular in Savannah, named America's Most Haunted City. Tours available every day of the year.

JEPSON CENTER FOR THE ARTS
207 W York St, Savannah, 912-790-8800
www.telfair.org/visit/jepson

The Jepson Center features over 7,500 square feet of gallery space, a 220-seat auditorium, and community center, education studios, and ArtZeum-a unique, 3,500-square foot interactive gallery for children and families. The Jepson Center is home to the Telfair's **Kirk Varnedoe Collection** featuring works by artists such as Jasper Johns, Chuck Close, Roy Lichtenstein, Jeff Koons, Frank Stella, and Richard Avedon.

The **Telfair Museum of Art**, the oldest art museum in the South, wanted to expand, and the result is a light-filled building that won praise for its architect, Moshe Safdie. When they built the Jepson Center for the Arts, the planners preserved Savannah's cherished street grid by dividing the structure into two, and joining it with two glass bridges, while giving the museum much-needed space. The original 19th-century museum (121 Barnard Street) is home to the **Bird Girl**, the now-famous statue that adorns the cover of "Midnight in the Garden"; it was moved from Bonaventure Cemetery for her protection. The museum also operates tours of the nearly 200-year-old **Owens-Thomas House** (124 Abercorn Street). Nominal admission fee.

JULIETTE GORDON LOW BIRTHPLACE
10 E Oglethorpe Ave, Savannah, 912-233-4501
www.juliettegordonlowbirthplace.org
The birthplace of Juliette Gordon Low, the founder of the Girl Scouts of the USA, is a beautiful house built in 1821. This architectural gem has become a destination for Girl Scout troupes.

MERCER WILLIAMS HOUSE
429 Bull St, Monterey Square, Savannah, 912-236-6352
www.mercerhouse.com
This historic house, located on Monterey Square, was built in the 1860s for the great grandfather of songwriter Johnny Mercer. This architectural gem was restored by Jim Williams, the antiques dealer made famous in the now-classoc book, *Midnight in the Garden of Good and Evil*. Mr. Williams survived three murder trials but he was indeed acquitted. Tour

guides tend to embellish the good part of the story as Mr. Williams' sister, Dorothy Kingery, still lives on the second floor where guests are not allowed. The guide will share descriptive details about the rest of the house, the formal courtyard, the nap-ready veranda, the Continental rococo and the Edwardian Murano glass.

NON-FICTION GALLERY
1522 Bull St, Savannah, 912-376-9953
www.nonfictiongallery.com **WEBSITE DOWN**
Non-Fiction offers artists a variety of ways to exhibit their work. The gallery features contemporary fine art and craft shows, local artisan pop-up shops, and gallery-sponsored juried shows. Students and emerging artists can also rent gallery space to showcase new work.

OATLAND ISLAND WILDLIFE CENTER
711 Sandtown Rd, Savannah, 912-395-1212
www.oatlandisland.org

Just five miles east of Savannah, this environmental education center holds such wildlife as endangered Florida panthers, eastern timber wolves and a variety of birds of prey. You can wander the nature trail which winds through Low Country forest and marsh. Programs for children are available.

OLD SAVANNAH TOURS
250 MLK Jr Blvd., Savannah, 912-234-8128
www.oldsavannahtours.com

Ghost Tours are a favorite in Savannah and Old Savannah Tours offers a 90-minute Ghostly Nights tour starting at 7 p.m. aboard an open-air trolley. Daytime trolley tours are also available through town. Riders are given a map and can climb on or off throughout the Historic District.

OLD TOWN TROLLEY TOURS
855-245-8992
www.trolleytours.com
Highlights the top Savannah attractions with 15 stops and more than 100 points of interest.

SAVANNAH TOURS
212-852-4822
www.savannahtours.us
They have a Paula Deen tour, but the most popular tour is the Historic Savannah Trolley Tour. This tour operates from 9 to 4:30, and you can hop on and hop off at 14 different trolley stops. This gives you the ability to explore Savannah at your own pace.

SHANNON SCOTT TOURS
330 Bonaventure Rd, Savannah, 912-319-5600
www.shannonscott.com
One of Savannah's most popular tours is that of the Bonaventure Cemetery and Shannon Scott's Journeys are more than a tour. Scott is a storyteller and has pioneered some of the city's first specialty tours and this one is one of the best. While he offers tours of the cemetery during the day, Savannah's number one tour is Bonaventure Afterhours where you are literally locked in the cemetery for 2 hours.

T. S. CHU'S
7726 Johnny Mercer Blvd, Savannah, 912-897-7795
www.chusmart.com
Chu's convenience stores are located throughout Savannah and Tybee Island. Not your typical convenience mart, here you'll find everything from car washes to beach rafts, sunscreen, fishing tackle and hardware.

TYBEE ISLAND LIGHTHOUSE & MUSEUM
30 Meddin Dr, Tybee Island, 912-786-5801
www.tybeelighthouse.org
A tour of the Tybee Island Lighthouse features a 178-step climb to the top but the breathtaking view is worth the effort. **The Tybee Island Museum** is located in Battery Garland. Choose a guided sunset tour and you'll see one of the most beautiful coastal sunsets in the world.

Chapter 7
SHOPPING & SERVICES

DID YOU FIND AN INTERESTING PLACE?
If you discover a place you think I should check out on my next visit, drop me a line, will you? I'll mention your name if I end up listing it.
andrewdelaplaine@mac.com

24 E STYLE DESIGN CO.
24 E Broughton St, Savannah, 912-446-1601
www.24estyle.com

Owners Ruel and Delaine Joyner offer a unique design shop set in a 1921 department store building, where customers can find handmade furniture from Indonesia and Hungary that can be ordered with custom upholstery designed by the owners.

A.T. HUN GALLERY
302 W Saint Julian St, Savannah, 912-233-2060
www.athun.com
A staple in City Market for over 16 years, this gallery offers a colorful and eclectic group of art from 25 local and international artists. Much of the art found here is untraditional and unique.

ALEX RASKIN ANTIQUES
441 Bull St, Savannah, 912-232-8205
www.alexraskinantiques.com

Located inside the Noble Hardee Mansion, a gilded, four-story Italianate home, this shop specializes in antique furniture of all periods but also offers a variety of items including architectural fragments, paintings, carpets, and accessories. You'll find everything from Louie to Lucite, rugs, carpets, paintings, and rare artifacts.

ARCANUM ANTIQUES AND INTERIORS

14 W Jones St, Savannah, 912-236-6000
www.arcanummarket.com/
This antique and interior shop offers a variety of furniture and design pieces. You'll find original art, antiques, and contemporary furniture. Design services available.

BACK IN THE DAY BAKERY

2403 Bull St, Savannah, 912-495-9292
www.backinthedaybakery.com
This relaxed bakery lives by their motto, "Slow Down and Taste the Sweet Life." The bakery offers handcrafted baked goods like cakes, brownies, artisan breads, pies, cookies, and cupcakes as well as lunch fare and excellent coffee.

BLICK ART MATERIALS

318 E. Broughton St, Savannah, 912-234-0456
http://www.dickblick.com/stores/georgia/savannahbroughtonst/
This two-story art supply store is popular among SCAD students and local artists. The first floor features art supplies from spray paint to oil paints as well as office supplies and unique toys. Upstairs you

find drawing paper, canvases, glue, portfolios, and a variety of bags and totes.

THE BOOK LADY
6 E Liberty St, Savannah, 912-233-3628
www.thebookladybookstore.com
Located in the center of the Historic District, this shop offers over 50,000 new and used books in over 40 genres. The shop also offers event like book readings and signings, free Wi-Fi, and book clubs.

BRIGHTER DAY NATURAL FOODS
1102 Bull St, Savannah, 912-236-4703
www.brighterdayfoods.com
This natural food store is the ideal shop for vegetarians and vegans offering great products, fresh organic produce, vitamins and supplements, a deli and juice bar, and an outdoor café.

CHOCOLAT BY ADAM TURONI
323 W Broughton St, Savannah, 912-335-2914
www.chocolatat.com
Adam Turoni, Savannah's very own Chocolatier, offers up some of the best chocolates available. The décor is a chocolate lovers fantasy and the floor is faux grass. A variety of chocolate choices are available from the typical to the unusual including peanut butter cups, red velvet, pumpkin truffles, habanero truffles, Mayan chocolate truffles and

Bailey's Irish cream truffles. This is a self-serve shop where you grab a tray and using a tong, select your favorite chocolates.

COPPER PENNY
22 W Broughton St, Savannah, 912-629-6800
www.shopcopperpenny.com
This boutique offers upscale women's fashions and footwear. Copper Penny collections feature a Southern sensibility and style. Here you'll find designer fashions, footwear, accessories and jewelry.

CUSTARD BOUTIQUE
422 Whitaker St, Savannah, 912-232-4733
www.custardboutique.com

This popular boutique carries a variety of fashions for women including everything from shoes and accessories to bags, designer dresses and gifts. Name brands offered include: French Connection, Super Maggie, By Boe, Tano, Gillian Julius, Jeffrey Campbell, ALL Black, and Miss Oops.

DAVIS PRODUCE
7755 U.S. Highway 80 E., 912-897-0802
https://www.facebook.com/pages/Davis-Produce/137652852924664?sk=info&tab=overview
If you're on your way to Tybee Island and want some fresh fruit to take to the beach, stop here. Or just grab a bag of boiled peanuts or a jar of salsa or pickles to take home. You can't miss this produce stand on Talahi Island, at Quarterman Drive and Highway 80 East.

E. SHAVER BOOKSELLER
326 Bull St, Savannah, GA 31401, (912) 234-7257

www.eshaverbooks.com

Located on Madison Square, this is Savannah's oldest bookstore. Here you'll find twelve rooms filled with fiction and non-fiction books. The shop specializes in local and regional topics such as history, architecture, decorating, arts, and cooking. There's also a section dedicated to the Civil War.

FABRIKA FINE FABRICS

2 E Liberty St, Savannah, 912-236-1122

http://fabrikafinefabrics.com/

Located in the heart of downtown Savannah, this fabric store carries sewing supplies for craftsman of all levels. The shop specializes in high quality natural fiber fabrics and hard to find notions. This is the only shop in Savannah that caries certain types of better apparel fabrics and PFD fabrics for dyers and printers. Classes in garment construction, quilting, and fun crafts are offered. SCAD fashion and fibers students shop for supplies here.

FOLKLORICO

440 Bull St, Savannah, 912-232-9300

No Website

This beautiful, unique shop offers a selection of gift items not found in chain stores. What you'll find here is a nice selection of international "folk" art from more than 30 different countries. The shop also carries artifacts, iconography, accent furniture, ceramics, pottery, blown glass, textiles and contemporary art.

FORSYTH PARK FARMERS MARKET
South End of Forsyth Park, Savannah
www.forsythfarmersmarket.com
Open daily from 9 a.m. to 1 p.m. (rain or shine), this farmer's market offers a variety of vendors selling produce, hand-made products, local goods including eggs, honey, pastured meat, bread, cheese, mushrooms, herbs, preserves, coffee beans and plants.

FRESH MARKET
5525 Abercorn St #60, Savannah, 912-354-6075
www.thefreshmarket.com
Fresh Market is known for offering the freshest quality products, both locally and internationally. The market has an old world charm and visitors shop while listening to classical music. Here you'll find high-quality meats, fresh seafood, and local, organic produce.

GALLERY 209
209 E River St, Savannah, 912-236-4583
www.gallery209savannah.com
Two floors of original art, woodworking, crafts, photography, jewelry, and gifts.

GLOBE SHOE CO.
17 E Broughton St., 912-232-8161
In the middle of one of the main streets in the touristy Historic District, this shoe store is loaded with flats, wedges and pumps by the high-quality shoemaker Stuart Weitzman. You'll also find cute shoes by Via Spiga, Ugg, Vaneli, Sam Edelman and Gentle Souls. Paula Deen shops here (well, she used to—now, her

assistants pick up shoes for her to try on—she's besieged with autograph seekers when she goes out).

GO FISH
106 W Broughton St, Savannah, 912-234-1260
www.shopgofish.com
This unique bohemian boutique features fashions, shoes and accessories including lots of hand-made, one-of-a-kind items from around the world. Here you'll find hippie style dresses and many items designed in-house by the owners.

GRAVEFACE RECORDS & CURIOSITIES
5 W 40th St, Savannah, 912-335-8018
www.graveface.com
A unique shop that sells new and used vinyl records, bitters, cocktail supplies, toys, games, taxidermy (how about a rabbit bust or a rat's skull or sick-looking dolls with fake blood dripping off them?), and performance equipment. Consignments available. This shop might even buy your old record collection. On-site video games – free play.

HALF MOON OUTFITTERS
15 E Broughton St, Savannah, 912-201-9393
www.halfmoonoutfitters.com
Since 1993, this shop has provided quality goods and services for adventure and travel. Here you'll find gear for paddle boarding, rock climbing, back packing, kayaking, trail running and other outdoor adventures. Look for name brands like The North Face, Patagonia, Mountain Hardwear, Smartwool and Keen.

HARLEY-DAVIDSON
1 Fort Argyle Rd, Savannah, 912-925-0005
503 E River St, Savannah, 912-231-8000
www.savannahhd.com
Here you'll find everything Harley-Davidson from motorcycles (new and pre-owned) to fashions, and accessories. Rentals, service, and even instructions available – home of Rider's Edge Academy of Motorcycling.

JERE'S ANTIQUES
9 Jefferson St, Savannah, 912-236-2815
www.jeresantiques.com
Since 1973, this shop has been a favorite of collectors, designers and auction houses. The owner maintains a warehouse in England with buyers working throughout Britain as well as in Belgium,

Holland and France. Owner Jere Myers maintains his own warehouse in England and has buyers and pickers working throughout Britain and on the continent in Belgium, Holland and France. With a constant supply of new inventory, shoppers can discover a variety of treasures like an 18th century chest, a 19th century breakfront or an Art Deco vanity.

KELLER'S FLEA MARKET
5901 Ogeechee Rd, Savannah, 912-927-4848
www.ilovefleas.com
Popular among locals and tourists, this flea market has over 400 retail stall spaces and six food concessions. The flea market has showers for traveling vendors, handicap access and a barbershop. Here you'll find a variety of unique, unusual, and even useful merchandise at bargain prices.

KOBO GALLERY
33 Barnard St, Savannah, 912-201-0304
www.kobogallery.com
Located adjacent to Ellis Square, this gallery features a co-op atmosphere with a group of local artists that include: Christi Reiterman, Daniel E. Smith, David J. Kaminsky, and Dicky Stone.

LEOPOLD'S ICE CREAM
212 E Broughton St, Savannah, 912-234-4442
www.leopoldsicecream.com
This beautiful store was designed by Academy Award nominated designer Dan Lomino and it's filled with props, posters, and signed photographs of actors. The shop includes much of the original 1935 décor including the original soda fountain, back bar, sundae holders, and banana split boats. A local's favorites because of the original, secret ice cream recipes.

MADAME CHRYSANTHEMUM
101 W Taylor St, Savannah, 912-238-3355
No Website
This beautiful shop offers a variety of flowers and gifts. You'll not only find amazing flowers but an assortment of things for the garden, candles, jewelry, stationary, and a few odds and ends for the house.

MALDOROR'S FRAME SHOP
2418 De Soto Ave, Savannah, 912-443-5355
www.maldorors.com
A frame shop with the aura of a Victorian curio shop, featuring antique prints, custom framing and woodworking.

OGLETHORPE MALL
7804 Abercorn St, Savannah, 912-354-7038
www.oglethorpemall.com
Oglethorpe is a regional shopping mall with a food court, a carousel, and a variety of name stores including: Belk, JCPenney, Macy's, Sears, Old Navy, Hello Kitty, and Stein Mart.

ONE FISH TWO FISH
401 Whitaker St, 912-447-4600
www.onefishstore.com
This shop exudes "coastal cool" with its eclectic inventory of trendy jewelry, LouenHide handbags, Pine Cone Hill linens, Archipelago Botanical bath and body products or Mariposa glossy pewter serving and entertaining pieces. And you'll fall in love with the cute honeybee embellishments on the straw or fabric handbags by Bosom Buddy Bags.

THE PARIS MARKET
36 W Broughton St., 912-232-1500

www.theparismarket.com
Owners Paula and Taras Danyluk travel the world and fill their fascinating little shop with goods they think you can't live without. You'll find Savons de Marseille blocks of olive oil soap (I love these great soaps) as well as small cotton bags of imported lavender. Downstairs you'll find a sprinkling of antiques and even vintage sacred items such as an old church altar, Madonna statue and Santa Rosa candles from Mexico. Here you'll find collections from Milan, Rome, Florence, England, as well as from the flea markets of Hungary, Holland, Belgium, and Paris. Here you'll find a world of treasures including everything from handbags, jewelry, architectural finds, teacups, perfume, and furniture. Local artists rotate their artwork through the shop.

PARKERS MARKET
222 Drayton St, Savannah, 912-233-1000
www.parkersav.com
Regional convenience store that combines a gas station with a Fresh Market.

PINCH OF THE PAST ARCHITECTURAL ANTIQUES
2603 Whitaker St, Savannah, 912-232-5563
www.pinchofthepast.com
This place is a treasure trove filled of chandeliers, doorknobs and other hardware from old homes.

PLANTATION JEWELS
502 E River St, Savannah, 912-667-4608
www.mkt.com/plantation-jewels

This shop features the handcrafted jewelry made by owners Paul and Jeanie Chance. Every piece comes with a Story Book telling the history of the item. The artists use antique glass shards, antique china shards, and antique buttons that they have collected to make wearable art.

RIVER STREET MARKET PLACE
502 E River St, Savannah, 912-629-2647
www.riverstreetmarketplace.com
Experience this unique open-air shopping market next to the river featuring more than 50 vendors. Vendors offer a wide range of shopping including photography, art, and unusual imports.

SAINTS AND SHAMROCKS
309 Bull St, Savannah, 912-233-8858
www.saintsandshamrocks.com
Located in the heart of Downtown, this shop specializes in Irish imports and Catholic gifts. This shop services the needs of Savannah's Irish Catholic community.

SAVANNAH BEE COMPANY
104 W Broughton St, Savannah, 912-233-7875
www.savannahbee.com
Befitting its name, here you'll find a variety of pure and naturally organic honey products and beauty supplies. You'll find products such as honey and comb, beeswax-centric bath and body products, mint julep lip balm, and a variety of luxurious beeswax-based body care products. There's even a honey tasting station up front.

SAVANNAH CANDY KITCHEN-CITY MARKET
318 E Saint Julian Street, Savannah, 912-201-9501
www.savannahcandy.com
All lovers of sweets come to this place because it's filled with homemade goodies like pralines or gophers — pecan clusters covered with caramel and chocolate.

SAVANNAH MALL
14045 Abercorn St, Savannah, 912-927-7467
www.savannahmall.com
Located on the south side of Savannah, this is an enclosed regional shopping mall with four anchor

stores: Bass Pro Shops, Burlington Coat Factory, Dillard's and Target.

SEVENTH HEAVEN ANTIQUES
3104 Skidaway Rd., 912-355-0835
www.antiquesinsavannah.com
This low-slung building on Skidaway Road is easy to miss driving by, but you'll want to make a U-turn for this stellar shop loaded with early American furniture, china and jewelry. Its odds and ends range from a math book from 1878 to an Italian Palumba accordion, not to mention a variety of clocks, Canton

blue china (circa 1850), colorful Majolica dishes (circa 1870).

SHOPSCAD
340 Bull St, Savannah, 912-525-5180
www.shopscad.com
Located in Poetter Hall, this shop is a showcase for items designed and created by the students of Savannah College of Art and Design. Here you'll find treasures like jewelry, painting, baby blankets, greeting cards, towels, sculpture, handbags, clothing, photography and pottery.

V&J DUNCAN
12 East Taylor St, Savannah, 912-232-0338
www.vjduncan.com
Located in the Historic District, this shop offers a unique variety of antique maps, prints and books. Here you'll find a vast collection of old engravings, mezzotints, lithographs, photographs, old books and books from Savannah authors like autographed copies of the classic "Midnight in the Garden of Good and Evil."

ZIA BOUTIQUE
325 W Broughton St, Savannah, 912-233-3237
www.ziacouture.com
If you're a fan of exotic jewelry you'll love this fashion-forward jewelry boutique. You'll find a nice selection of handmade exotic jewelry and accessories from 48 different designers from around the world. There's sterling silver and gold, unique home accents, gemstones, and handbags.

INDEX

1

17HUNDRED90 INN, 12

2

24 E STYLE DESIGN CO., 71

4

45 BISTRO, 25

7

700 Drayton, 18
700 DRAYTON, 25

A

A.T. HUN GALLERY, 72
A-J's DOCKSIDE RESTAURANT, 26
ALEX RASKIN ANTIQUES, 72
American (New), 36

AMERICAN LEGION SAVANNAH POST NO 135, 54
American Traditional, 48
ANDREW LOW HOUSE, 58
Aqua Star, 22
ARCANUM ANTIQUES AND INTERIORS, 73
ARCHITECTURAL ANTIQUES, 84
Association of Historic Inns of Savannah, 12
ATLANTIC, 27

B

BACK IN THE DAY BAKERY, 73
BAKERY, 28
BALLASTONE, 12
Barbeque, 47
BATTLEFIELD PARK, 59
BED AND BREAKFAST INN, 21
Bird Girl, 64
BLICK ART MATERIALS, 73
BLUE ORB TOURS, 59
BOAR'S HEAD GRILL & TAVERN, 28
BOHEMIAN HOTEL, 13
BOOK LADY, 74
BRICE, 13
BRIGHTER DAY NATURAL FOODS, 74
BULL RIVER MARINA, 60

C

CANDY KITCHEN-, 87
Casimir's Lounge, 18
CASIMIR'S LOUNGE, 55

CAT, 8
CAT Shuttle, 8
Chatham Area Transit, 8
CHOCOLAT BY ADAM TURONI, 74
CLARY'S CAFÉ, 29
CLUB ONE, 55
CONNECTONTHEDOT, 9
COPPER PENNY, 75
CRYSTAL BEER PARLOR, 56
CUSTARD BOUTIQUE, 75

D

DAVIS PRODUCE, 76
DECK BEACH BAR AND KITCHEN, 30

E

E. SHAVER BOOKSELLER, 76
EAST BAY INN, 14
ELIZABETH ON 37TH, 31
EMPORIUM KITCHEN AND WINE MARKET, 32

F

FABRIKA FINE FABRICS, 77
FERRY, 9
FLANNERY O'CONNOR'S CHILDHOOD HOME, 61
FLYING MONK NOODLE BAR, 33
FOLEY HOUSE INN, 15
FOLKERICO, 77
FORSYTH PARK, 61
FORSYTH PARK FARMERS MARKET, 78

FORT PULASKI, 61
FOXY LOXY CAFÉ, 33
FRESH MARKET, 78

G

GALLERY 209, 78
GALLOWAY HOUSE B&B, 16
GEORGIA STATE RAILROAD MUSEUM, 62
GLOBE SHOE CO., 78
GO FISH, 79
GRAVEFACE RECORDS & CURIOSITIES, 79
GREEN FIRE PIZZA, 34
GREEN TRUCK PUB, 35
GREY, 36
GRYPHON TEA ROOM, 37

H

HALF MOON OUTFITTERS, 79
HARLEY-DAVIDSON, 80
HEARSE TOURS, 63
Heavenly Spa, 22
HUSK, 38

I

Italian, 45

J

JEPSON CENTER, 63
JERE'S ANTIQUES, 80
JULIETTE GORDON LOW, 65

K

KEHOE HOUSE, 17
KELLER'S FLEA MARKET, 81
Kirk Varnedoe Collection, 64
KOBO GALLERY, 82

L

LADY AND SONS, 40
LEOPOLD'S ICE CREAM, 82
LIGHTHOUSE, 70
LOCAL 11 TEN FOOD & WINE, 41

M

MADAME CHRYSANTHEMUM, 82
MALDOROR'S FRAME SHOP, 82
Mansion on Forsyth Park, 25
MANSION ON FORSYTH PARK, 17, 55
MARSHALL HOUSE, 18
MASADA CAFÉ, 42
MERCER WILLIAMS, 65
MONTAGE AT PALMETTO BLUFF, 18
MRS. WILKES' DINING ROOM, 43

N

NON-FICTION GALLERY, 66

O

OGLETHORPE MALL, 83
OLD SAVANNAH TOURS, 67
OLD TOWN TROLLEY TOURS, 68
OLDE PINK HOUSE, 44
ONE FISH TWO FISH, 83
Owens-Thomas House, 64

P

Pacci Italian Kitchen & Bar, 14
PACCI ITALIAN KITCHEN + BAR, 45
PARIS MARKET, 83
PARKERS MARKET, 84
PLANTATION JEWELS, 84
PLANTERS INN, 19
PRESIDENTS' QUARTERS INN, 19
PUBLIC TRANSIT, 8

R

RANCHO ALEGRE CUBAN, 45
RIVER STREET INN, 20
River Street Pedestrian District, 7
Roundhouse Railroad Museum, 59

S

SAINTS AND SHAMROCKS, 85
SANDFLY BBQ, 46
SAVANNAH BEE COMPANY, 86
Savannah Belles Ferry, 9
SAVANNAH MALL, 87
SAVANNAH TOURS, 68
SENTIENT BEAN, 47
SEVENTH HEAVEN ANTIQUES, 88
SHOPSCAD, 89
SIX PENCE PUB, 48
SOHO SOUTH CAFÉ, 48
Southern, 43
STREETCAR, 9
SUNDAE CAFÉ, 49

T

T.S.CHU'S, 69
TAVERN, 57
Telfair Museum of Art, 64
THUNDERBIRD INN, 21
Tybee Island Museum, 70

V

V&J DUNCAN, 89
VAN GO-GO'S, 49
Vietnamese, 33

W

WALKING, 9
WALL'S, 50
WESTIN, 22
WILDLIFE CENTER, 67
WYLD DOCK BAR, 51

Z

ZIA BOUTIQUE, 90
ZUNZI'S, 52

WANT 3 *FREE* THRILLERS?

Why, of course you do!
If you like these writers--
Vince Flynn, Brad Thor, Tom Clancy, James Patterson, David Baldacci, John Grisham, Brad Meltzer, Daniel Silva, Don DeLillo
If you like these TV series –
House of Cards, Scandal, West Wing, The Good Wife, Madam Secretary, Designated Survivor

> You'll love the **unputdownable** series about Jack Houston St. Clair, with political intrigue, romance, and loads of action and suspense.

Besides writing travel books, I've written political thrillers for many years that have delighted hundreds of thousands of readers. I want to introduce you to my work!
Send me an email and I'll send you a link where you can download the first 3 books in my bestselling series, absolutely FREE.

Mention **this book** when you email me.
andrewdelaplaine@mac.com